MONIQUE ESCAPES

Édouard Louis

MONIQUE ESCAPES

Translated from the French by John Lambert

HARVILL

1 3 5 7 9 10 8 6 4 2

Harvill, an imprint of Vintage, is part of the Penguin Random
House group of companies

Vintage, Penguin Random House UK, One Embassy Gardens,
8 Viaduct Gardens, London SW11 7BW

penguin.co.uk/vintage
global.penguinrandomhouse.com

Penguin
Random House
UK

First published by Harvill in 2026
First published with the title *Monique s'évade* in France by Éditions du Seuil in 2024

Copyright © Édouard Louis 2024
English translation copyright © John Lambert 2026

Typeset in 12.5/18 pt Bembo Book MT Pro by Six Red Marbles UK, Thetford, Norfolk
Printed and bound in Great Britain by Clays Ltd, Elcograf S.p.A.

The authorised representative in the EEA is Penguin Random House Ireland,
Morrison Chambers, 32 Nassau Street, Dublin D02 YH68

A CIP catalogue record for this book is available from the British Library

ISBN 9781787305045

Penguin Random House is committed to a sustainable future
for our business, our readers and our planet. This book is made
from Forest Stewardship Council® certified paper.

'It is thus the New Life which I see.'

Hélène Cixous, *Eve Escapes*

I

She called me in the middle of the evening. She was crying. I was twenty-eight at the time of the call and it was only the third, maybe the fourth time since I was born that I'd heard her cry.

She told me on the phone that the man she'd met after her break-up with my father and with whom she was now staying in a caretaker's flat in the centre of Paris was putting her through the same things, repeating the same behaviour that my father had inflicted on her for twenty years, only worse; he drank, a lot, when the sun went down he poured himself glass after glass of whisky in old mustard jars that now served as drinking glasses, and once he'd had a drink he'd start insulting her, calling her

a slut,
a whore,
a cunt,

I could hear him behind her as she spoke, that evening in February, he insulted her even as she was talking to me on the phone, I was witness to it, I could hear this man telling her that she was nothing but a slut, a whore, that her son – me – was nothing but a faggot, that her other sons – my brothers – were just plain losers and now she couldn't stop, she couldn't hold back her tears, she told me, *I freed myself from your father, I thought this would be a new life for me and now it's starting all over, everything's starting all over again,* she said, her words interspersed with sobs, *I don't know why I have such a shitty life, why I only meet men who stop me from being happy I mean I don't deserve to suffer this much,*

did I do something bad?

I started crying too.

Her crying made me cry.

I struggled to catch my breath. I sat down on the sofa behind me and said: 'Don't worry, we'll find a solution' – words dictated by the circumstances, heard no doubt hundreds of times in films or on TV; it's always in the most dramatic situations that our reactions are the most conformist.

I tried to think as fast as I could: 'Okay, I know what we're going to do. You're going to put some clothes in a bag and leave now. You're going to go to my place.'

She could take refuge in my flat; I didn't want her

staying with a man who was aggressive with her and made her suffer, she had to leave without delay, a friend in Paris who had the key to my flat would come and let her in, of course I hadn't told my friend yet but I knew he would, I knew he'd help me out – help her out. I explained to my mother that I'd been out of the country for several weeks and would be away for another two because of professional commitments, that I couldn't come back to France at the drop of a hat but would do my best from a distance.

She answered:

'I don't think I have the strength to leave now anyhow. I'll leave tomorrow.'

I insisted: we couldn't know how things would develop if this man she was living with was so aggressive that evening. What if he became physically violent? What if he tried to hit her? Or if he suddenly threw himself at her? That's not so rare, I told her, you remember how my sister came home with bruises on her face made by a man, Loïc the football player I found so handsome, you remember that my brother hit a woman until she ended up calling the police, all my life and especially in our family I've seen men who hit women, and I don't want that to happen to you, I told her, *I don't want that to happen to you, you've got to leave, you've got to leave*, and all the time I was trying my best to convince her, the man

behind her kept bawling, Why're you looking at me like
that, you think I'm going to be scared just because you're
whining about me to your son,

you bitch,

you cunt,

you think I'm going to be scared of your fucking son,

and hearing him insult her like that, I said to her, You
see, listen to how he talks to you, I can hear everything,
you've got to get out of there, my friend Didier will
come help you, please listen to me Mum, just take some
clothes and your dog and leave, please just leave, but she
answered with all the fatigue of a wounded animal in
her voice, she didn't speak, she breathed, *No, no, I can't
leave just like that, I've got documents I can't leave here, important papers, I'll wait until he's asleep and then pack them up, he
knows he's got me because all my things are at his place.*

I begged her: *Documents are nothing, you can renew them,
we'll renew them, I promise, you can declare them lost and we'll
get them renewed, just go, go*, I said: *If you called me it's because
you felt you were in danger, otherwise you wouldn't have done it,
you have to leave tonight*, but all my begging was useless, she
wasn't going to change her mind, I even got the feeling I was
insisting too much, and all of a sudden I was afraid, afraid
of making an already suffocating situation more difficult, I
started to feel bad, and I stopped trying to bring her round.

I sighed:

You're sure it won't be too hard to get through the night if you stay?

She took a deep breath. She'd stopped crying:

'One more bad night isn't going to change things. Anyway soon he'll be so drunk he'll fall asleep and let me have some peace. Don't worry, I'm used to it.'

I knew she was used to it. All through my childhood when my father was drunk I'd seen him call her

Fat cow,

Fat heap

or just Fatso, above all in front of other people, to make them laugh and to humiliate her. I knew she was used to it, I just wished she could put that behind her.

She repeated:

Don't worry. I'll be all right. I'm sorry I phoned you.

I made her promise to leave the next day, as soon as she could, and she promised. I asked her:

'Do you want me to stay on the phone with you? I can stay here all night if you want.'

But she refused.

'No. If he sees me talking to you he'll get even angrier. I'll just ignore what he says to me until he's so drunk he falls asleep.'

I hung up, then wrote to Didier. When his name

showed up on my phone screen, I answered and told him what had just happened. Didier said he could be at my place at any time the next day to open the door for my mother and give her the keys. I asked him if he could withdraw some money and advance it to her so she could do some shopping, buy some food and basic stuff and that I'd repay him when I returned to Paris and Didier said of course, of course he would.

I put the phone down, looked around the room and waited. I don't know what I was waiting for.

★

I tried to spend the evening as normally as possible. I couldn't. I was certain that a catastrophe was about to happen. I wrote to my mum on WhatsApp: You okay? Things aren't getting out of hand?

She answered: Things are fine. Go to sleep, don't worry. I imagined her cowering in a corner of the living room while the man next to her screamed; I imagined the light from her phone reflecting off her face as she tapped on the keyboard, the shades of green and purple on her skin causing her to appear and disappear. I remembered reading in a history book that one day the skeletons of Neolithic women had been found with their bones broken by the violence of men. The violence my mother was experiencing bore the smell of prehistoric caves and caverns, the smell of violence dating back tens of thousands of years.

I asked: Is he sleeping now? I waited for her answer.

I got up, paced up and down.

Was I making too much of this? Was I exaggerating? Or was it that she'd been through so many scenes like this one that in the end she was able to adapt better than I could, even though she was the one being attacked and insulted, and not me?

Was she lying to me about how serious things actually were?

I suspected she was.

I remembered how my sister showed up one evening when I was a teenager with bruises on her face, and her lie that no one believed: *I hit my head again man am I a spaz.*

I remembered the stories my father used to tell about his father – my grandfather – who'd hurl chairs at his wife's head when he was drunk, stories she – my grandmother – never told.

Did my mother also keep certain things unsaid?

Finally she wrote back: 'Okay, he's gone to sleep. Tomorrow I'm leaving, I swear. Go to sleep.'

I forced myself to believe her; I took a sleeping pill,

went to bed and left the ringtone on. I didn't want to miss a call from her, any news at all. I was afraid of an accident, I dreamed of a miracle.

★

The next day. She'd waited for me to wake up and appear online on WhatsApp, and wrote: 'I'm ready.'

I protested, 'Why didn't you let me know you were awake?' She replied: 'I wanted to let you get some rest.'

All night I'd been afraid she'd go back on her plans. I'd had nightmares of her calling me to tell me that she'd changed her mind, that she was going to stay after all; I told her that but she seemed sure of her decision:

No, it's over. I'm not going to let people walk all over me any more, I'm leaving and that's that.

The man she was living with was still sleeping, it was the perfect time to leave. She'd searched through the drawers and got together all the documents she didn't want to leave behind: her family record book, her social security card, her prescriptions. Her ID. She'd packed a small bag with T-shirts, socks, a single pair of trousers in addition to the ones she was wearing; when I'd talked to her the day before about her escape and sketched out a plan, I'd recommended that she take the bare minimum of things to avoid lugging too much stuff around and hurting her back.

I'd thought that a heavier suitcase could have made her escape more difficult, slower, and that the man she was living with could have heard her, made out some noises on the stairs, woken up and caught her, the scene had gone round and round in my head like a vision of horror, I'd imagined this man putting his hand on her shoulder and saying, *Where're you going like that? You're not going anywhere*, and she, petrified, unable to move because of her enormous suitcase, would then be locked away by him, watched so that she wouldn't attempt any more escapes, I described this scene to her, my fear that it would come true but she repeated that all she had was a backpack, a tiny backpack that was easy to sling on, and her dog.

So everything was ready.

'Time to go?'

'Yes, time to go.'

I ordered a taxi for her in Paris from the flat where I was staying in Athens, thousands of kilometres away from her tired body, from her trembling breath.

Less than five minutes later the driver informed me that he was downstairs. She went down:

'I'm leaving.'

She was leaving behind years of her life, clothes, things she'd bought over time to make the flat less gloomy, as she said.

I pictured her five-foot-two body breaking out onto the street, her backpack slung over her shoulders, her tiny dog under her arm, her hurried stride as she crossed the space between her building and the car that was waiting for her, her breath, her breath, and I imagined her repeating, inwardly: I'm not going to let people walk all over me any more. That's over.

I called Didier to let him know that she was heading over to my place; he too was already on his way. He hadn't waited for my signal, he'd suspected how things were unfolding and had got a head start.

On the screen of my phone, a miniature black car symbolising the taxi progressed through the different neighbourhoods of Paris, with my mother inside. I squinted as if I could get a brief glimpse of her, as if by dint of concentration I could turn that symbol into a living, moving thing.

She was leaving.

★

She'd been living in Paris for seven years. When she talked about it she said to me, quite often: 'I can't believe I live here! In Paris! That I've started a new life at my age, over fifty!'

She'd spent the biggest part of her existence in an isolated village in the north of France, the one where I'd grown up with her, a village with barely a thousand inhabitants, far from everything, for so long she'd seemed condemned never to leave, yet one day she'd done it: she'd defied her destiny.

It was in this village that she'd met the man she'd have to flee seven years later, the one who'd enabled her to escape in the first place. She – my mother – had just kicked my father out after more than twenty years of marriage, twenty years during which he'd expected her to cook,

clean the house,

do the shopping,

hang out the washing,

wash the dishes,

and keep quiet while he watched TV, six or seven hours a day, or risk him exploding,

in the end she couldn't stand this atmosphere any longer and miraculously she'd managed to kick him out.

After this break-up, she'd lived alone with my little brother and my little sister, and several times a week, at the end of the afternoon, she'd get together with her neighbour in the garden next door to drink lychee liqueur or little glasses of whisky.

There, during one of these ritual cocktails, facing the sun that was setting in the distance behind the factory smokestacks, a man had appeared. He was the neighbour's cousin. He was from the region but had been living in Paris for the last ten years or so, in one of the chicest districts of the capital: he worked as the caretaker of a building. He looked at her and smiled, he had a go at seducing her; she didn't resist, they slept together and after they'd seen each other on and off for a few months she went to live with him in Paris, where I was studying.

The first time I saw her again, in a little street near the Seine, she'd done her hair and put on make-up; she was smiling; I'd never seen her so *self-aware*. I could see from the look on her face how happy and amazed she was at what she was experiencing. It's important to understand: most of the women she and I had known in the Nord department lived and died in the same village, or moved only a few kilometres away, they spent their lives with the same husband, even when they no longer loved him: they stuck it out. But not my mother. Not her. It was this pride that I saw on her face that day. She'd quipped: 'You see how beautiful I am now that I'm living here,' and I'd quipped back: 'Yes, it's true, you're beautiful. You're the queen of Paris.'

She didn't know, and I couldn't have known either, that this dream would be so short-lived.

★

This too: as she was getting into the taxi, the morning of her escape, I remembered the day when I'd promised her that we'd spend an evening together in a restaurant near the Eiffel Tower. Shame is a memory. I remembered because I was ashamed. It was the third or fourth year after she moved to Paris, I hadn't seen her for several months and I'd written to tell her that this evening together would give us a chance to get back in touch and have a good talk. She replied almost instantly:

'Great! What time?' and I suggested:

'9 o'clock?'

But at the end of the afternoon, a photographer who was passing through Paris invited me to have dinner with him and I accepted. I wrote to my mother to tell her that I had a problem, something had come up at the last minute, an important professional meeting. I lied. It wasn't a professional meeting, it wasn't important, I was just naively flattered by the idea of having dinner with a world-renowned artist rather than her.

She wrote back just one word:

'Ah.'

Then another message, a few minutes later: 'Too bad, I got all dolled up' – since she'd left my father and moved to the big city, *getting dolled up* had been her revenge on life, a way of reappropriating her body and not being reduced to the status of a domestic slave: 'To think that I spent years in T-shirts and tracksuit bottoms scrubbing the floors in a dump in the middle of the countryside while your father watched TV, without ever doing a thing for myself, all that's over now.'

Now that I knew what she'd put up with at the hands of this man she'd been staying with in Paris, that he drank, insulted her, was aggressive towards her, I thought back to how I'd cancelled our evening together and I was paralysed with shame. I understood that a date with someone, whether the one with me that had got her hopes up or any other, must have represented an escape, however brief, from the reality of her daily life.

An outside.

Later she'd tell me: 'It had been like that with him for a long time, but I didn't tell you because I didn't want to worry you.'

Later my shame would continue to grow, to take up more and more space inside of me.

★

But to continue: she crossed the city in the taxi with her dog on her lap, her backpack on the seat beside her. A woman escaping. Sitting there in Athens, I followed the car's progress through the streets of Paris on my screen.

Didier was already at my place; ten minutes later he heard her coming up the stairs, slowly because of her weight and her shortness of breath from asthma and cigarettes.

She came into the flat, her forehead glistening with sweat. Didier said to her: 'You're courageous. It's no easy thing to run away. I admire you.'

She repeated it to me on the telephone the next day: 'Your friend told me that I was courageous. And that he admired me. You could tell he meant it.'

In her life, my mother often clung to the compliments she received; they gave her and still give her the feeling of finally being seen, of existing in the eyes and words of others, and so of breaking with the invisibility imposed on her by poverty and her life with men who were set on crushing her. When I was a child, she'd sometimes repeat to me several times a day how someone had complimented her in the supermarket or the town square, and I'd get annoyed. I'd shout: 'You've told me that a thousand times!!!'

Now I understood.

Didier took her backpack, put it on the table and stayed with her for a few minutes, they talked a bit; but he was afraid he'd tire her out. That evening he'd tell me that she seemed very weak and he didn't know if he should stay or go, keep her company or leave her to herself. He'd said that to her, quite simply, he wanted to do what was best for her, and she whispered: 'Yes, I think I need to rest.'

He gave her the sum I'd asked him to advance, in addition to a few groceries he'd bought for her, he told her again that she could call him any time she wanted, and left.

When he let me know that he was going home, a new image came into my mind, that of my mother in the silence of my flat, between two lives, somewhere between a past to be escaped from and an unknown future.

I don't know if I found this image beautiful or tragic, beautiful because my mother had just freed herself, or tragic because she'd have to start all over again, free herself once more, she who'd thought her happiness had been guaranteed forever since she'd left my father.

How many times had she said to me after that break-up: *I'm going to be free at last!*

She wasn't. She was still going to have to fight.

Didier wrote to me: 'She's going to need you, I think.'

I looked at the time, weighing things up in my mind. I should give her time to settle in, I thought; I counted, five minutes, ten minutes, then I called her by video to check how she was doing.

'Are you okay? It's not too tough?'

Her voice was hoarse:

'I'm fine. I'm tired but I'm fine.'

I felt tears come to my eyes again when she said that. Tiredness had always been the central sign of injustice in my mother's life. Tiredness at being reduced to the domestic sphere, tiredness at being humiliated, tiredness at having to run away, tiredness at having to fight, tiredness at always having to start all over again.

There are people who are carried along by life and others who have to fight against it.

Those who belong to the second category are tired.

We stayed on the phone for a long time, talking by video call; she described how she'd got her things together and packed her bag, how she'd waited for the man she was living with to fall asleep, collapsed in a drunken stupor on the sofa, how, even as his eyes were closing and he began to doze off, he'd continued to insult her, out of sheer habit. She'd forgotten some important things in her rush, things that meant a lot to her and that she'd have liked to have with her, as well as all the clothes she hadn't been able to take, and I tried to reassure her by promising that I'd send a friend over to get them.

She was hungry; I offered to order a meal and have it delivered so she wouldn't have to cook or wash dishes. The idea of her doing household tasks in this context upset me.

'I'll order your meals every day and have them delivered, until you get back on your feet, okay? It'll be our little ritual. We'll try out different restaurants, Indian food, Lebanese food.'

Was I overdoing it again? I asked her, but she stopped me:

'I'm shattered, I don't mind doing as little as possible.'

There was another thing: I was afraid she'd get bored at my place. She'd been parachuted into a foreign environment, alone, surrounded by the books I'd accumulated over the past few years. Above all there was no TV in my flat and I knew she watched TV a lot, particularly to while away the time in the afternoon.

That was no big deal, she said, she'd watch a film on her phone; anyway she had a headache, she couldn't concentrate on a thing.

A short silence followed, she looked around the room and I understood that I should let her rest. I said:

'Okay, I'll call you back tomorrow. Try to relax a bit now.'

'Yes, I'm going to have a lie-down. I think I'll sleep all day, get up, eat and go back to sleep.'

'Mum?'

'Yes?'

'I want you to know, I'm proud of you.'

★

Barely a year after she moved to Paris, she'd knocked on the door of this same flat, in the middle of the afternoon. I was startled; nobody ever comes to my place like that, without warning.

I'd been writing; I closed the lid of my computer and went to open the door. It was her.

I asked:

'What is it? You can't just turn up at my place when I'm working without letting me know, that's not okay, I have to stay focused.'

She said apologetically:

'I won't bother you for long, I just want to use the toilet.'

I looked up at the ceiling:

'Sure, fine . . .'

I waited for her to come out of the bathroom and sit down. I'd poured her a glass of orange juice.

'Why didn't you just go to a café? You order something to drink and use the toilet, it's simple.'

(I didn't dare tell her that things were different in the city than in the country, that in the city it's taboo and practically unthinkable to knock on someone's door, even someone you know well, without telling them in advance.)

She replied:

'I couldn't go to a café.'

'Why not?'

'Because I don't have any money.'

She explained that by moving in with the man she was seeing, she'd lost the benefit payments she'd received following her break-up with my father, and that in coming to Paris she'd also left behind her part-time job, which together with the benefits had given her a certain independence.

By following a man, she'd become dependent.

'And when we argue he tells me that for all the trouble I cause him he won't give me a cent more. So I don't even have a euro or two to order a coffee and go to the toilet. Today I wanted to go for a walk and I wandered too far from our place. So I had to come here, otherwise I wouldn't have bothered you.'

I'd forgotten this scene, and suddenly I remembered. Shame is a memory.

★

The day after her escape, eleven in the morning. I'd just woken up. I drank a couple of coffees and called her:

'How are you today?'

She looked like she was out of breath, as if she'd been running.

'I'm still tired, but I'm okay. I slept a lot. I'm glad I left.'

That reassured me; I'd started to worry again that she'd regret her escape and go back.

That had worried Didier too: 'Now that she's got the hardest part behind her, she needs to hang in there and not go back to that man. It takes so much energy to escape and break free that often, right when you've almost made it, you give up and go back.'

Didier was right, it's often easier to put up with the suffering you know than to surrender yourself to a new situation. It'd already happened once; when I was eight or nine years old she'd made a first attempt to leave my father.

She'd called her sister who came to get us – my mother, my brothers and sisters and me – and we all went to live in her flat in the city, which reeked of plastic when the linoleum on the floor was warmed by the sun's rays. But two or three days later, my mother announced that we were going home. My father had called her and begged her to come back, and she'd given in: how could she have got by, with no money, no qualifications, no driving licence, no vocational training, alone with five children?

Later she'd say about this moment in her life: 'I'd have liked to have left, but to go where? And how would I have managed?'

I'd dreamed of a life without a father, and felt betrayed: I was too young and didn't yet know that freedom has a price, a price my mother couldn't pay.

★

So that morning after her escape I asked her once again:

'You're not going back to that man, you promise?'

She answered:

'No way, I've got my freedom, I'm keeping it. I promise.'

I switched to a lighter subject:

'So what will you do today? Any ideas?'

She shrugged.

'Go shopping with the money your friend Didier left

me, walk the dog . . . I don't know. I admit I don't know what to do.'

I felt bad when she said that. If I'd been there with her we could have gone for a walk, taken in a film or drunk cocktails in a hotel bar to take her mind off things – when she moved to Paris, for the first few weeks I'd taken her to the most luxurious hotels in the city, the Park Hyatt, the Ritz, the Plaza Athénée, places I'd never have thought of going to under normal circumstances. I'd wanted to share some unforgettable moments with her to celebrate the start of her new life, to take her to places that were over-the-top beautiful and inaccessible, and I remembered how much she'd loved these brushes with a luxury she never thought she'd even get a glimpse of, and how she'd said as she raised her glass and recalled that just a few years earlier she was still living with my father in a run-down house in a village in the Nord department:

'We're not doing too badly, are we?'

This time that wasn't going to be possible; I apologised for being so far away, I'd signed a contract for a writing residency in Athens and I needed the money that came with it. In any case, it was thanks to this residency that my flat was free and she could stay there until we found a more lasting solution – although today I can't help wondering: should I have gone back? Were there other things

I could have done but didn't do? How much of what I remember am I reconstructing now?

I said to her:

'Look, Mum, you're going to get bored at my place if you don't have anything to do. I'll call a friend and ask him to come and install a television, but in the meantime you can use my computer to watch films and series.'

She bit her lower lip.

'I don't know how to do that, I don't have a clue, you know that.'

I hadn't thought about this, it had slipped my mind: my mother had never really used a computer.

'I can show you by video.'

She resisted, still looking exhausted, her voice trailing off:

'Never mind, I'll watch stuff on my phone . . .'

I insisted:

'It's not that complicated, I promise. If you're bored you'll be unhappy. And if you're unhappy, you'll be tempted to go back . . .'

I suggested calling her back in a couple of hours to give her time to take a shower, get dressed, and have some breathing space. She could use it to think things over, and if she didn't feel like it we'd let it drop. I hung up and went out for a walk in the streets, the sun outside was strong, it forced me to close my eyes.

★

As an aside: my mother had never learned to use a computer, just like she'd never been able to learn to drive or undertake any professional training.

All of these absences in her life were part of the same system.

When she was seventeen and she got pregnant for the first time, she stopped her training as a cook to bring up my brother. As for her first husband, he didn't stop his apprenticeship.

Later when she wanted to get her driving licence, my father talked her out of it: he said that she didn't need it because he had his, all she had to do was ask him and he'd take her where she wanted to go – which of course he didn't.

When she could have been learning how to use a computer she lacked the time because she was
preparing breakfast for the children every day,
waking them up for school,
ironing their clothes,

picking them up when classes were over – *in fifteen years I never saw my father do any of these things*.

She'd never done a single thing for herself.

Until now, her life had been a life for others.

★

Her face reappeared on the screen of my phone. She'd put on glasses as if she was preparing to do something serious.

'You ready?'

'Yes, I'm ready. I'm at the computer.'

I joked:

'You're cute with your little glasses.'

And she laughed:

'You're dumb . . .'

'OK, let's be serious, here we go.'

The first thing to do was turn on the computer. It took her a few seconds to find the button I'd described then I heard the sound indicating that she'd succeeded, the login screen appeared. I started: *So, I'm going to spell out my password. Can you hear me? The first letter is capital M.* She repeated my words, more hesitantly and stretching out the vowels, *Sooo, ooookaay, the fiiiirst leeetter, caaapitaaal M.* She stopped:

'How do I do capitals?'

'You press the shift key and the M at the same time.'

She made a slight nasal sound.

'Umm, where's the shift key?'

Short silence.

Hesitation.

This was going to be more difficult than I'd thought.

'You see keys the furthest to the left on the keyboard? The shift key should be the second or third from the bottom, a big arrow pointing up. The keypad must be about the same as the one on your phone when you send a message.'

She couldn't find it. She said:

'There's no key like that . . .'

And I answered:

'Yes there is, Mum, look carefully.'

'I swear there isn't.'

'Yes there is . . .'

Short silence.

Hesitation.

'Ah, there it is!'

I finished spelling out the password which she typed in letter by letter:

'And now you press enter.'

The same thing happened as with the shift key.

'Enter?'

'Yes . . . It's one of the keys on the far right, also big, it should say Entrée or Enter on it.'

She looked:

'Uh . . .'

Then she sighed and took off her glasses:

'I'd rather stop, we can do this another day.'

I insisted:

'Come on, you can do it. And once you get the hang of it, you'll be able to do it your whole life . . . You managed to leave an alcoholic, you can start a computer.'

She laughed again and I laughed with her.

'Let me remind you that I didn't leave one, I left three. I've had three husbands. Three drunks.'

'All the more reason to believe you can use a computer. Ready to try again?'

She rubbed her eyes.

'Ready.'

She took a deep breath and we continued, step by step.

I told her to open a browser window, to move the mouse across the screen, but she didn't understand what these terms meant. I said, *Double-click, Close this page*, but she didn't know the meaning of any of these words, any of these expressions; I'd never thought about it, suddenly I realised how much technical vocabulary you need to master just to connect to a website.

I took out the laptop I'd been using in the flat in Athens and demonstrated what she had to do, bringing the camera close to my fingers to show her the gestures and actions she should repeat.

Her eyebrows furrowed, she whispered, *Okay, Yes, Got it.*

She sighed, dispirited, the tiredness from her escape the day before came back into her eyes, I felt guilty for dragging her into this situation, but she picked herself up; she hopped up and down on her chair a few times, shouting: *I did it the first time! Talk about a talented woman!*

After almost half an hour, she managed to open the homepage of a streaming platform.

She put her glasses down on the table in front of her and whispered: *Done.*

She was fifty-five and together, through the screen that separated us, we were trying to make up for all the years that had been stolen from her.

★

When she put her glasses down on the table, she didn't just say: *Done.* She also said: *I love you my son.*

I didn't know what to respond.

★

My embarrassment awakened my memories and reminded me of the time when my sister's son came to spend a long weekend with my mother in Paris. He'd turned six the week before and she wanted to use the occasion to show him her new life, her neighbourhood, her brand-new habits – it was just after she'd moved in.

During this little holiday together they did all the things you'd expect of a city break: they walked along the streets near the Louvre, strolled through department stores, ate ice creams outside the cafés in the Jardin du Luxembourg and the Tuileries. On their last evening together I met up with them near the Odéon Theatre and asked my mother:

'Arthur's going home tomorrow, right?'

She was holding his hand, and suddenly she got a lump in her throat:

'Yes . . . He's leaving tomorrow I'm going to miss him . . . I'm happy when he's around.'

Her emotion took me by surprise, threw me off balance: when I was a child I'd never seen her well up like that when she said goodbye to one of my brothers or sisters. I'd never seen her be so gentle, so sentimental.

In my childhood, when I lived with her, my mother was a rather hard woman. Everything my father put her through plunged her into a permanent state of oppression and anxiety, which transformed her into someone who was often cruel. I can still see her smoking a cigarette in the dark corners of the house and badmouthing the neighbours or her own children. For years, I remember, I dreamed of another mother, of having another mother instead of my mother, more tender, more loving.

But after she left my father and moved away, she changed.

The dividing line was clear, precise: there was my mother before the break-up, and there was my mother after the break-up, like two distinct people. And she wasn't just gentler after this transformation: she also became funnier, more understanding of others.

She was aware of this metamorphosis.

Later she'd tell me about her separation from the man she'd lived with in Paris: 'I wanted to leave before he made me as mean as your father made me.'

★

It was the second day after her escape across the city in a taxi. She seemed like she was doing better, her face was changing. During the day she'd explored the neighbourhood with her dog and watched a film; she told me she liked this rhythm where she was in charge. Where she didn't have to take account of anyone's wishes but her own.

The man she'd escaped from called her several times a day, he left her voicemails, in some of them he begged her,

Come back honey I miss you,

in others he'd get angry, shout, hurl insults,

What in christ's name are you doing?

You think you're clever running off like that,

he demanded explanations, he didn't understand why she'd disappeared, he wanted to know where she was.

'I delete his messages as soon as I get them. And you know what? It's good to hear him begging like that.'

The money I'd asked Didier to give her from me had almost all been spent, she'd used it to buy the basics that were missing at my place, dog food, shampoo, coffee, washing-up liquid, fruit; I transferred money to her bank account, then we sketched out a little summary of the progress she'd made so far: she'd regained her strength, she felt better, she had things to eat and ways of passing the time, she was sure she wouldn't go back; she dreamed of making a new start.

So the next step was to figure out where she was going to live. I'd already tried to ask her the day after her escape but she'd sighed, not in annoyance I think but in bewilderment, and she'd said with a lost look on her face, as if begging me to stop asking questions, *I don't know, I don't know.*

Now I thought the time had come to talk about it; I'd have to come back from Athens eventually and even if that hadn't been the case, she was going to need a place *of her own*.

'Have you put some thought into it?'

She nodded:

'Yes, I have. I thought maybe I could go live in the village your sister has moved to. It's pretty there and I could see her children . . .'

It was an excellent idea; not only could we find a house there for the same price as a tiny flat in Paris or in the suburbs, but above all my sister would be more available to see her and spend time with her than me – I had to face the facts, in the few years we'd been living in the same city I'd only seen her about ten times, no more.

'You're right, that could be a good move for you. Do you want us to start looking at some estate agents' websites?'

She approved:

'You could take a look, and if you find something nice you can show me. Would that be okay?'

I said that would be fine, and offered to make a first selection and send it to her.

★

During these few days of escape and preparation for her New Life, my mother required *total* care. She felt that after what she'd just been through she was entitled to rest and *radical assistance*, and I agreed, I was happy to do it – years earlier Didier had done the same for me when I'd been bedridden for days after an operation. He'd brought me my evening meals, called me almost every hour, given me books, kept me company until nightfall, I was basically reproducing with my mother what friendship had taught me, she – my mother – basically felt, as I too had come to feel, that emancipation does not come only through action but also, in some cases, through a right to abandon oneself, to delegate, to withdraw.

★

I started looking for a house for her. I logged on to estate agents' websites, downloaded applications, typed 'house to let' and the name of my sister's village in the Google search bar. I scrolled down the pages but nothing appeared; I didn't understand. To gain time I cancelled appointments that had been scheduled in connection to my residency, saying that I was held up by my writing work, and returned to the applications, I repeated the search but without specifying any price or size to get as many results as possible, then I tried again with the name of a neighbouring village, manually selecting the area on the maps proposed on the various websites, but each time the same message appeared: 'No property matches your search.'

I kept trying, using other tactics, on other sites. I don't want to exaggerate, and yes, sometimes one or two places did turn up, but the photos showed either a house in ruins, or a gigantic country house too far away from my sister's village, nothing resembling a place where my mother could have lived – and for the first time I got a feeling of the importance of the expression *to live* somewhere, and not just to stay there: to find a place where her life would be liveable, and not just a shelter or a roof over her head. She hadn't lived with the man she'd lived with. She'd stayed with him, but that very cohabitation had made her life unliveable. I have to be careful with the expressions I use, he wasn't *the man she'd lived with, he was the man she'd stayed with.*

I called Didier to ask him what he thought. He said I should try calling an agency in the region and I called the one in the nearest town, about twelve kilometres from the village.

A man picked up the phone.

He asked me a few questions, then explained to me that

the best thing would be to look 'on site', as he put it: in a village that small you can find a house to rent by talking to people in the neighbourhood or in the town square, he said, sometimes by taping an ad up in the window of a bakery or a café, but not on the Internet, apart from a few exceptions the sites I'd visited only listed houses for sale – how could I have forgotten something so basic after growing up in a village and knowing full well how things work there?

'Is there someone you know who might be able to go and ask around, maybe at the town hall or in the shops?'

I said in a low voice:

'Mmhmm, yes, my sister lives there . . .'

She'd moved to the village three years earlier with her husband and her two children, I knew that from my mother, but I hadn't spoken to her in eight years.

She'd been angry with me when I published my first novel, a book in which I wrote about our family, and in particular about the poverty and violence we had experienced – her as much as me. She sent me insulting messages the day after the book came out, and then nothing; I never spoke to her again after that, but I still had her phone number.

I thanked the agent for his advice, took a deep breath and called my sister.

'Hello?'

'Hello?'

I tried to imagine her face from the inflections in her voice. Had she changed?

'Can you hear me? It's me.'

'Édouard?'

'Yes. You all right?'

'I'm okay. It's been a long time . . .'

'True . . .'

There was no anger in her voice. More like sadness and nostalgia. It's strange, anger would have made me feel more at ease.

I didn't know what to say, so to get over the embarrassment I announced in a hurried voice, *Look, I need to talk to you about something.*

I explained the situation, my mother's escape, the new existence she needed help building, the house that was nowhere to be found.

She already knew some of what I was saying. She listened, made suggestions; I had the impression that at any moment she could have interrupted me to ask me to explain the eight years of silence between us, but she didn't.

She offered to call me back in a day or two, after she'd had a chance to ask around at the shops near her home and talk to the people she saw every morning taking her children to school.

I thanked her, hung up and wrote to my mother: *I'm still looking, Clara is helping me. It's a bit more difficult than I expected.*

★

I'd been close to my sister, a long time ago. When she was fifteen, she'd started doing part-time shift work in a small bakery in the centre of the village where we grew up. Then when she finished middle school she started working there full-time; she'd dreamed of becoming a Spanish teacher, but the careers adviser had discouraged her, telling her that in a region as deprived and poor as the Nord department it was better to be pragmatic and start working right away, rather than risk studying.

She'd leave very early every morning, before sunrise, to put the bread and pastries on the shelves, and get back home in the early evening.

My parents insisted she give them half her salary every month to help pay for the family expenses, and she felt that was unfair: she knew girls, her friends, who worked like she did and whose parents didn't ask them to pay a thing; they used the money to buy video games, clothes, phones.

So when she was seventeen or eighteen she left, and moved into a fifteen-square-metre studio in a street near the bakery. She often invited me to come and stay with her, most of the time in a text message she'd send me late at night, when everyone else was asleep. I'd stick some things in a backpack, leave a note for my mother on the table and walk through the streets to join her, the only sound my footsteps on the asphalt.

I'd spend two, three nights with her.

I remember we'd sit on the sofa and watch series all afternoon in her tiny room, and criticise our parents, in fact we said a lot of the things I'd later write about them – that's the main reason I wasn't at all expecting her reaction to the book when it came out. I remember we went to nightclubs in the evenings and sang at the top of our lungs in the car, and to the supermarket on Wednesday or Saturday afternoons, for hours, or whole days buying clothes or bottles of pop, I remember we laughed in the huge, air-conditioned aisles that smelled of pre-packaged food and floor detergent.

From the day I started to go to university, something no one in our family had ever done, from the day I started reading books, going to the theatre, getting interested in the history of cinema, all of those things suddenly became impossible. All at once I was bored, I hated the afternoons in the supermarket, I considered them a waste of time, I despised video games and found them stupid, I started saying – because I'd heard someone say it on campus – that the smell that hung in the air in fast-food restaurants was disgusting, that it made me nauseous.

I stopped spending afternoons or nights with my sister.

I knew her less and less well, even before we stopped seeing each other altogether.

That's also a form of class distance, of class violence: no longer being able to sing together in a car, no longer being able to laugh together in the aisles of a supermarket.

★

Two days after our first conversation in eight years my phone rang. I answered; it was her, my sister. I could hear a smile in her voice:

'Good news, I've found a couple of things.'

She'd looked everywhere it was possible to look, in the shops, at the town hall, on residents' Facebook groups, she'd asked everyone she knew and even the people she only knew from crossing paths in the morning on her way to work who she didn't usually talk to, and her efforts had paid off, she'd found two places where my mother could possibly live: a studio above the village bakery, and a small house with a garden, in a quiet street on the edge of town. She sent me photos of both places as she spoke. I swiped through the pictures and said I had to hang up, I wanted to call my mother and tell her, I couldn't wait.

During the two days my sister had spent looking for a place, my mother had started to dream:

'Can you believe it, I'm fifty-five and I'm going to live on my own for the first time in my life!'

When her face appeared on my phone screen, I shouted:

'We're almost there! There are two places! One's bigger than the other but they both look really good.'

She shouted just as loud as I did:

'Let's hear! I want to know everything.'

How many times had we shouted together in our lives, rather than at each other?

I filled her in on what my sister had said and asked her if she wanted to see the photos of the two places. Yes, she did. She wanted to see them immediately. She didn't know how to look at pictures she received while she was still talking on her phone, so I hung up, gave her five minutes and called her back.

'What do you think?'

'I really like them.'

We had to act fast: my sister had given me the number

of the village solicitor, he was the one in charge of organising viewings.

If he confirmed that it would be possible to see the house and studio quickly, I could send my mother a train ticket from where I was in Athens, and she could meet up with my sister and compare the two places with her.

'How does that sound?'

'Good.'

I let two or three seconds go by:

'All this moving around won't be too tiring for you, when you're just starting to recover?'

It had only been five or six days since she'd escaped, maybe she didn't want to or didn't have the strength to bustle around and make such important decisions.

But once again I was wrong, she was all in:

'Oh no, I'm up for it, I'm not going to complain when it's time to look at places to rent! Can you call the solicitor and let me know what he says?'

I nodded, *Of course I can.*

Before I hung up she asked me:

'Can you show me a bit of Athens?'

I walked over to a window and opened it so she could see the white stone buildings outside, the pale concrete and the metal sheeting that form the cityscape and which that day, like almost every day of the year, reflected the sun. I promised her we'd go somewhere soon. That we'd take a trip, together.

★

Why did I feel such a deep need to help her?

★

I called the solicitor. He could arrange a viewing of the studio and the house two days later. He spoke in a polite, friendly voice.

I told my mother and booked train tickets for her and her dog — and all the while this question in my mind: *why did I feel such a pressing need to help her?*

I kept phoning her at regular intervals as we waited for the time to pass before the viewings; she wanted to talk.

Like many people who've escaped from a violent situation, she wanted to tell her story:

'You know he'd been doing it for a really long time. Drinking too much and becoming mean every time he drank. When I got involved with him things were still okay, he drank at dinner, but then he started drinking earlier and earlier every day. At six in the evening, then at four, then at three. And in the end he'd already be completely plastered in the afternoon. He'd criticise me, but mostly he'd attack my children, especially you. He'd say, Your son's just a faggot, doesn't that make you want to puke? And I couldn't stand him insulting you. You can attack me but not my children.'

She told me:

'He was nasty about money too. He was the one who wanted me to come to Paris, he was the one who got me to give up my flat in the Nord department and move in with him. I'd hesitated . . . I'd thought to myself: if things go badly I'll be stuck there with him. I'd told him that, he'd said, Come on, you'll see, it'll be nice, I'll take care of you. But of course I'd been right to have my doubts. When he was drunk he'd lay into me, You're living here at my expense, let me remind you. If I took some butter from the fridge he'd say, Take less butter than that you can see you're not the one who's paying. If I made myself some hot milk he'd say, Half a cup of hot milk is enough, you don't need a whole cup. I'd tell him, You're the one who pestered me to come and live here, don't forget, but he wouldn't listen to me, he'd start up all over again, Anyway I've had enough of you and your family, and your loser sons, you see what they're like your kids, an alcoholic a slacker and a faggot and as for you you're just

a bitch

a cunt.'

I sighed:

'That's all over with now. Don't give it another thought. In a couple of hours you'll be visiting your new home, and soon you'll be far away from him.'

★

I woke up earlier than usual on the morning of the viewings and waited for her call.

I had a meeting with the actors of a Greek theatre company for a work session linked to my writing residency, and I went.

Crossing the city, arriving at the theatre, muted voices.

I don't remember a thing. I didn't listen to what was being said to me. I was thinking about my mother, about the places she was viewing, about her new life. All the rest seemed unimportant. Even today all the rest seems unimportant compared to this one thing: life, its possibility.

In the middle of the afternoon I received a video call and I found a place where I could tuck myself away; this time it was both of them, my mother and my sister, who appeared on the screen. I rediscovered what my sister looked like; she hadn't changed much in eight years. The same features, just a little more tired. She spoke first:

'Okay, we've had a look at the studio and the house. Did you get the videos?'

Yes, I'd got them and watched them.

'The studio is just above the bakery. It's small but very pretty, and it's in the centre of the village, where the shops are. The house has two bedrooms upstairs, a little yard and a garage. It's bigger, so of course it's more expensive.'

I asked the price of both:

'The one above the bakery is 320 euros a month. The other is 480, so it's a bit too much for Mum, I think.'

My mother cut in:

'It's too bad because the house is really quite nice, with a little garden. It would have been ideal for my dog . . .'

My sister turned to her and frowned.

'But with the money you've got, it's not realistic. How are you going to manage?'

My mother shrugged.

'I know, I was just saying . . .'

I suggested we could look at the photos and videos again with a clear head, and reflect on it; an hour later I called my sister back; I'd waited until she was alone to spare my mother the impression that her fate was being decided by others right in front of her:

'Are you sure we can't get the house for her? She'd be so much happier. I think she's suffered enough up to now . . .'

'I agree, but Mum doesn't have any money . . .'

'We could give her a little every so often, you and me. So she can have the house and some outside space for her dog. Okay, she doesn't receive much in benefits, but she'll get by, and maybe she can find the odd job . . .'

My sister made a sad, reflective face.

'Really I can't, I've got my children to look after . . . I could go shopping for her sometimes if she moves here, buy her food when she needs it, but I can't give her any money.'

I insisted:

'Not even forty or fifty euros?'

'No, I can't . . .'

I thought about it and said:

'Look, I'll take care of this.'

*

What my mother had seen as a betrayal was now what enabled us, together, to build her freedom.

Like my sister, she'd resented me for writing a book

about my childhood and our family. But paradoxically it's because I'd written that book, and the ones that followed, that I'd earned the money we could now spend on her.

After talking with my sister I thought of Jamaica Kincaid and her great novel dealing with her brother's death. In it, Kincaid recounts how all her life her mother reproached her for studying and writing books, but it was because she became an author, a status that gave her access to a more privileged existence, that she was able to buy hard-to-get medicine for her dying brother.

Jamaica Kincaid writes: 'Had my life stayed on the path where my mother had set it, the path of no university education, my brother would have been dead by now. I would not have been in a position to save his life, I would not have had access to a medicine to prolong his life, I would not have had access to money to buy the medicine that would prolong his life.'

It was the same thing, the same situation that was playing out with my mother: what she had seen as a betrayal now enabled us to face the present. What she had experienced as violence towards her was now going to free her from violence.

★

I called her back to tell her that I'd talked it over with my sister and if she wanted to, she could move into the little house with the garden, I'd help her out.

She hesitated:

'Are you sure? You don't have to . . .'

I repeated:

'I'm sure. Now I want you to be happy.'

★

She went back to Paris after the viewings. My sister had a lot of work and she didn't want to disturb her.

'So did you enjoy your little expedition?'

She nodded.

'A bit more tiring than I thought it was going to be, but I'm happy.'

'And what would you like to eat for dinner tonight?'

I asked because I was getting ready to order dinner for her, as had become our routine since her escape.

She replied in a playful way, like a countess talking to an underling, in the tone she used when she wanted to amuse me:

'I don't know my dear, what do you suggest for me this evening?'

I scrolled through the options on my screen, the

brightly coloured dishes arranged and photographed against a neutral background to catch people's eye.

'Hmm, that depends on what you'd like. Lebanese cuisine?'

I could tell she liked the idea.

'Oh yes, I've never had it.'

I asked:

'Never? Hummus? Falafel? Haricot beans in tomato sauce?'

'No, never.'

The exclusion that had formed the fabric of her life had played out in such tiny, tiny details, I thought as I listened to her: at over fifty she's never yet appreciated certain flavours, never experienced certain tastes, like a form of culinary and sensory deprivation. When we think of deprivation, of poverty, we think of not being able to buy clothes or pay bills, but we don't think of these things, flavours, smells, sensations that you've never known.

One by one, I read out to my mother the names of the dishes on offer and the descriptions beside them. She hesitated, changed her mind, I gave her some tips.

When I clicked to confirm her selection she stretched her arms towards the ceiling:

'I'm happy to try new things.'

In those few days, even something as trivial and banal as ordering a meal online became an act of revenge.

★

I also joked with her:

'When you get the house above all don't let a man move in with you. You're done with men. Now when you want one we'll pay a professional for a night but no more commitments.'

She giggled into the camera:

'In that case I want a Brazilian, with shoulders this big,' she spread her hands in an exaggerated way. 'Or a Swede, with beautiful blue eyes.'

★

Five more days and I'd be able to return from Greece. I'd just confirmed the choice of the house to the solicitor, who was in contact with the owner and informed him straight away. The owner agreed that my mother could move in a week later.

I announced to her:

'In a week you'll have your own home!'

I'd spent quite a long time talking through all the practical details with the solicitor, he accepted that I could pay the first four months' rent plus the deposit. That way my mother wouldn't be held up by the sluggishness of the authorities, as she would have been if she'd applied for financial aid for the move.

She wouldn't have to be anxious about money; she could spare herself that worry and focus on her wishes, on herself.

I asked her how much she'd need to live for the first few months. She thought about it, added up her daily expenses, I listened to her, she said, *I don't know how much it's going to cost me to shop just for myself I'm not used to it, it's going to be strange doing it just for me, I've spent my whole life shopping for a family or for men who were all big eaters, I don't know, let me think*, and as she spoke I thought: *For the first time she can say I and not We when she's planning her future*.

★

I could also put it this way: it's because I'd suffered in my childhood that I wrote books that led to conflicts with my family which paradoxically enabled me to help my mother escape and reinvent herself.

I could say:

No suffering in my childhood = no books published = no money = no freedom possible.

I could say that suffering and freedom are two moments in a single process, two movements in the same score.

I could say finally that I've never known a freedom that was not at the same time a deliverance from violence, and therefore also, in a way, an extension of it.

★

Worries and money. In my mother's life I'd always seen them go hand in hand.

When I was a child and she was always afraid that a bailiff would come and take the furniture to repay our debts, the unpaid rent, the electricity bills piled up in the letter box.

The words she repeated again and again,

uttered in the soft light of the wood-burning stove,

uttered in the cold and fog of the Nord department,

her words transformed, crystallised in the form of mist escaping from between her lips: *They're going to take the furniture, they're going to take the furniture*.

(It never happened, but it was always *about to happen*, in the sense that it was always on the horizon, always approaching us, far or near, never there but always there, constantly threatening.)

When she was worried because her children — because I — went to school in shoes with holes in them and she couldn't afford to buy new ones.

When she said: The shame that'll be heaped on us again, what are people going to say about my kids.

When fights broke out between us because I was hungry when I got back from school and she told me to stop taking the food from the fridge, when she shouted, when she got wound up,

Stop stuffing your face like that for chrissake!

and which I experienced as a personal attack, as an act of malice aimed at me, a plot against my stomach, without seeing that it was really because if I ate everything in the fridge there'd be nothing left for dinner that evening or the next day, nothing in the sense of nothing, total absence, nothingness, the nothing that people from privileged classes can't understand, because when they say they have nothing left, they always have something left,

they still have diplomas,

they still have culture,

they still have a few coins,

they still have their contacts to help them,

they still have the drive that privilege confers,

I've seen privileged people say *I've got no more money* in a restaurant and pay the bill a few minutes later, I swear, they don't know the meaning of the word NOTHING, of NONE or of NO MORE, of the word ZERO, but my mother knew that if I ate something when I got back from school she wouldn't be able to feed the rest of the family, although I was incapable of seeing or understanding that, it took me more than twenty years to understand, and I'm sorry, I'm sorry.

When she waited for me to come out of the toilet and shouted:

Stop using so much toilet paper! It's two sheets each time, you don't need any more!

and I felt persecuted.

When she shouted at me through the bathroom door:

Stop showering for so long!

and I felt persecuted, and couldn't see that it was because of money worries, and I said *We're not even allowed to wash in this fucking family*, and I hated her.

(I told her about these worries on the phone a few days ago and she said: *It was worse than you think. I used to talk about it with your father at night in the bedroom, in the dark, I'd say: What're we going to do? How're we going to eat? How're we going to get by? We'd get into arguments about it, him and me, but I hid it from you, you don't burden children with things like that.*

What else happened in the early years of my life that I hadn't been able to see? How many years does it take to start becoming aware of the reality behind your childhood?)

★

Didier sent me messages asking how my mother was doing. I kept him up to date on all the stages, all the issues and all the progress, as well as all the difficulties: the house that had been so hard to find, my sister's help and our unlikely cooperation after years of silence, the viewings, the money.

I said to my mother: 'Today I told my friend about what you did,' and she replied, astonished and flattered: 'Is that true? He asked about me?'

Didier told me about his own mother, who'd died two years earlier. She'd met his father when she was very young, just twenty. They moved in together, he worked in a factory and she was a domestic cleaner, they had children, it was her who looked after them, who cooked for them, who took care of everything at home. His mother was born almost forty years before mine, that is almost two generations earlier and yet for decades her life had resembled my mother's almost point by point.

She too had tried to escape her destiny, she took typing lessons, but she'd had to give up for lack of time and money. Later she started divorce proceedings, Didier told me, but then she backed out. She hated her husband, she couldn't stand his anger, his fits of jealousy, she would have liked to run away but she'd never been able to.

For years Didier's mother had lived a life that she didn't want to live, in a space from which she couldn't escape: her existence had been, to a large extent, a *prison existence*.

Listening to Didier I wondered: would his mother have left if she hadn't been a cleaner? If she hadn't been so poor? Are economic constraints enough to explain, for her or for others, at least partially, the impossibility of escape?

Didier wrote about his mother in the book he dedicated to her life and death:

'How was it that she convinced herself not to try to change her life? Or rather, how did the scale of the problems of all kinds she would have had to confront in order to live on her own, or her resignation faced with the sad destiny that she perceived as being hers, manage to convince her not to try to escape from this situation by any means possible? My mother, who at the time was a cleaner, had given up in the face of the hardships she would have had to confront had she decided to move out: How to cope with living alone with two children (we were under the age of ten)? How to leave everything behind, find an apartment, earn enough money each month to pay the rent and buy everything else we needed? "How would I have done it?" she repeated over and over during our conversation about this, as if trying to persuade herself that there was no reason to regret the decision she had made at the time, even if it was obvious that she couldn't help dreaming about what her life might have been had she followed through with these plans.'

As I read these lines I wondered: to what extent could money have enabled Didier's mother to escape?

Of course there are also other factors that make escape impossible or unthinkable – habit, fear of a violent reaction – but that's also the point: could money be enough to allow someone to overcome these factors of paralysis and renunciation?

Would it be possible to establish something like a price for freedom, a price that could be quantified rationally, mathematically?

Once this price had been set and the funds made

accessible to as many people as possible, would new escapes take place and multiply ad infinitum?

To put it more explicitly and so even more bluntly: how many people, how many women would change their lives if they got a cheque?

★

And I thought: these questions wouldn't arise if money, if inequality didn't exist. It's these more general problems that need to be addressed, and perhaps abolished. But first I have to save my mother.

And I thought of the words of the philosopher Georg Simmel: 'Assistance is based on the structure of society, whatever it may be; it is in open contradiction to all socialist and communist aspirations which would abolish this social structure.'

And I thought: But the category of assistance presupposes a belief in the idea of property. You can't think you're helping someone unless you consider that what you give is yours and yours alone.

But I wasn't helping my mother, because I believed that what was mine was also hers, and because of that there's a flux, a continuity in our destinies.

And I thought: Stop thinking! You have to act first, think later.
   Failing that no one would ever escape.
   Anywhere.

★

Eight years before her escape. I'm in the basement of a Paris bookshop, on a little podium, sitting in front of a group of strangers who've come to listen to me, students, women – I don't recognise anyone.

I talk about my first novel, the one my sister insulted me over, the one that made her – my mother – angry.

I bring up the harshness of my parents during the first years of my life, it seems to me that I say: *My father was violent with my mother and she was violent with us, as if she had to take out on others the burden she was suffering*, it seems to me that I say: *Suffering doesn't make you better, on the contrary*, I remember for sure that I talk about racism, about the hatred of homosexuality, and suddenly a silhouette stands up in the middle of the audience: it's her, my mother.

I hadn't seen her. She wasn't yet living in Paris, it was a year before she moved there, I'd never have imagined she could be there. I'd been answering a journalist's questions for over an hour, I'd spoken about her and she'd listened to everything.

The journalist turned to the room. He asked: 'Does anyone have a question for the author?' and it's at that moment that she stood up.

She'd waited, patiently, and now she was facing me, ten, maybe fifteen metres away, staring at me with an expression of reproach and vengeance, her hand raised exaggeratedly, outstretched, to show that she wanted to speak.

My temples began to throb, my cheeks burned – *how to react?*

I got up, left the room and took refuge in a storeroom tucked away at the back of the bookshop. It was all I could find to get away from my mother: I ran.

One of the organisers came and joined me.

'Is everything all right? Why did you leave the room?'

'That's my mother. That's her out there.'

She raised one eyebrow and frowned with the other: 'Ah . . .' Then: 'Okay, I think I get the picture. Don't worry, I'll be back in a sec.' Two minutes later, she returned and told me that my mother was waiting in an office, I could go back into the room to finish the event with the audience and decide whether or not to see her afterwards. She had agreed to wait for me but there was an emergency exit I could use if I preferred to avoid a confrontation.

I thanked the woman – I've never forgotten her

tenderness, her discretion – went back onto the podium, answered the last questions from the journalist and the audience, then headed for the office where my mother was sitting.

I'd decided to talk to her.

Seeing me come in, she shot me a furious look.

'Why did you do that? Why did you write a book to say that we were violent?'

'Isn't it true? Didn't Dad say that fags should be killed?'

'He said that as a joke . . .'

'A joke? And it never occurred to you that there are people who could be hurt by that?'

She changed the subject:

'And why did you say we were poor? You never lacked anything.'

'Mum, we were poor.'

'I've never neglected my children.'

'It's not the same thing.'

'I've always protected my children.'

'That's not true.'

She shrugged.

★

In less than a week, then, she was going to be able to move in. She needed furniture for the house. When she'd viewed it she'd seen that it was only partially equipped, 'semi-furnished' according to the rental agreement that the solicitor had sent me by email and on which I'd faked her signature *(the same scene again; I'd called her up:*

'The solicitor sent me the lease, I need you to sign it and send it back to me.'

She'd said:

'Can you take care of that? You can fake my signature you spent all of secondary school forging absence notes and skipping classes. Don't think I didn't notice you little rascal.'

I'd laughed. Those days marked by her escape were also marked by laughter, it must be said).

Furniture: talking to her on the phone I thought that soon her escape would no longer be just a word, it would be a reality we could brush with our fingertips, something solid we could feel under our palms; it would become palpable.

I asked her:

'What do you think you'll need for the house? We could take care of that together.'

She hesitated:

'I'd like to get the bedroom furniture and kitchen table back from the Guy. They belonged to my mother, I don't want to give them to him. He'll go to war to keep them after so many years in his flat, but I won't let that happen.'

I felt a slight grimace form on my face:

'Are you sure you want to go down that route? Maybe it's better to avoid a conflict, especially over furniture.'

'No, it's my mother's furniture, it's sentimental. I want it back. I'm not letting him have it.'

I tried to come up with an argument she'd be open to, words that would get through to her – I was afraid a conflict would put her in danger, there was no telling how this man would react when he saw her again, since she'd left he'd been leaving her messages that were sometimes aggressive, she'd told me, and I thought that emptying his flat on top of that wouldn't be the best strategy for calming him down; generally speaking, during that period I was more afraid than she was.

'Come on, memories of your mother are more important than objects, I'm sure she would have agreed with me. She'd have told you to think about yourself and not about nails and planks of wood.'

I pleaded with her, insisted about her mother, but I could see, it was like when I tried to convince her to leave without her documents and prescriptions the night before her escape, none of my arguments could make her change her mind.

'It's my mother's furniture, if he thinks he can keep it he's dreaming. Anyway that's my business.'

'But Mum . . .'

'Don't worry, I know what I'm doing.'

I understood that I had to let it drop.

'Right . . . So what would you need to be comfortable in your new home?'

She drew up a list: chairs, a fridge, a stove with an oven, a washing machine. And a vacuum cleaner. Together with what she was planning on getting back from *the Guy* – that's what she called the man she'd been staying with – and the sofa my sister had promised her, she'd have everything she needed to settle in.

'And your sister also said she'd buy me the little day-to-day items, tea towels, knives and forks. She even bought me a vase this afternoon she sent me a photo.'

I had an idea while listening to her:

'How about ordering the furniture you need straight away? Why wait?'

She was reticent:

'I don't want to ask too much . . .'

I smiled:

'You're not asking since I'm the one who's offering.'

She closed her eyes, as if to think, then she whispered: *Let's do it.*

I logged onto a website selling household goods and saw that some of the things she needed could be delivered in two days' time, maybe we could give my sister's address, she could receive the first packages, store them at her place or in her garage and bring them over the day my mother moved in.

'Not a bad idea. I'll call your sister.'

She hung up, called my sister who told her that would be fine, and rang me back.

I sent her images of the chairs and appliances. I took screenshots and shared them with her a second later, she switched from the video call to look at the images as soon as she got them, I'd shown her how to do it the day before, and said, *Yes, No, That one's better, That's a good idea, No.* I confirmed her choices, kept looking, put what she liked in the virtual shopping basket, deselected what she didn't want. The questions we asked each other were so practical and banal, did she prefer gas or electricity for cooking, did she need a freezer and if so, how many compartments, and yet, talking over these tiny details moved me deeply, because they were the most tangible manifestation of her future freedom, because freedom is also a matter of details.

My mother was totally thrilled, she spoke loudly, cracked jokes: 'The cooker can't be too big so I'll have an excuse never to cook for other people again', 'If they can deliver a cleaner with all that I'll take one!'

She evoked old memories, the present of her escape

gave new meaning to the past: 'I need a gas cooker with a good flame, that's the only way I can make poor man's stew. You remember poor man's stew? I'd put in potatoes and whatever else was in the fridge, all the old stuff that was lying around and shout: Tonight it's poor man's stew!'

We kept going like that, comparing appliances, reading reviews on specialised websites, checking out price differences between the shops, and after just over an hour the order was complete and confirmed.

Everything would be delivered two days later, three at the most.

When I was young, my favourite video game was one where you put together the entire life of an imaginary person. Each game began the same way: a tiny character, either a man or woman, landed in an empty plot covered with grass, with a small sum of money, some clothes and a letter box. From there, the aim of the game was to create a life for the character: find them a job, build a house and lay tiles or wood floors, buy furniture and plants.

Together, that day, with these screenshots of fridges and washing machines, we were putting together a life for my mother. Like in a video game, a reality without limits. As if everything were possible.

★

In the office of the bookshop where I'd had my talk with her, we said a few last things and went our separate ways. Little by little I started seeing her again after that, and her anger subsided, but I've never forgotten her look when she stood up in the audience, her look that is her rage and sadness.

★

'Okay, we're good, I can return home from Athens at last, the day after tomorrow.'

This was forty-eight hours after we ordered the appliances on the Internet. She smiled:

'When I see you I'm going to give you a big hug!'

There were just a few things left to be sorted out. I transferred the sum we'd agreed on to her account so that she could be self-sufficient for the first months of her new life; I called the bank to insure her house against theft and fire; the banker asked me to estimate the value of all the belongings that would be moved in; I asked my mother, I called the bank back; I phoned a van hire company to organise the move, my mother thought we'd need a van to pick up her things from the Guy's place, her clothes, her pictures, the furniture she was sure she'd be able to get back from him – and with each new step, new problems arose: what type of van would we need? How big? How much stuff makes up a cubic metre, how many boxes? Do you need a special licence to drive certain vans? I'd never driven before, never tried to get a licence, I had no idea. I called my sister for help and advice; I also wanted to know if she'd be willing to pick up the van with her husband, I'd seen that it was possible to hire one from a company near her home, they could drive to Paris, pick up my mother and her things, then drive back up north with her; she agreed; I needed a copy of her driving licence to send to the hire company as a guarantee; I called a friend and asked him to join us on the day of the move to help my sister, her husband and me carry the boxes; I bought the boxes over the phone and asked my mother if she'd like me to pick them up at the shop – how many would we need, ten, twenty? And how many rolls of tape? Would we need gloves to protect our hands from paper cuts from the cardboard?

Finally, at my mother's request I printed out a civil union dissolution form, so that she could break her civil union pact with the man she'd been staying with, and I called a lawyer in Paris to ask what would happen if the man she'd been staying with, staying not living, refused to sign.

There was only one thing left for her to do: call him,

the Guy, to tell him it was over, she was taking her things and leaving. She was leaving his flat and leaving him.

She hadn't said anything to him yet, he didn't know that in the days she'd been away she'd been secretly planning a break-up: he thought she'd simply been keeping her distance for a few days, a few weeks, but that she was going to come back. She called him, and called me back an hour later.

I hadn't been able to do a thing while waiting for her call, I'd been pacing up and down to stop myself from thinking.

'Hello?'

'Hello?'

That was that. The news had come as a shock, she said.

'He couldn't believe it, he was so taken aback that he couldn't even get angry. He cried on the phone.'

The truth is that she didn't feel sorry for him. She was happy to have shaken him up.

'Did he really believe he could do whatever he wanted to me and I'd just remain servile? Who does he think I am?'

I congratulated her:

'That's the spirit, you're strong . . .'

She was flattered and I was happy she was.

She had another piece of good news: he'd agreed to

let her take back her mother's table, wardrobe and bed, contrary to what she'd imagined, and above all to what I'd imagined, he hadn't put up any resistance on that score – or on any other for that matter, the surprise of the separation had stunned him.

I let her finish and said:

'Fine, I say we do the move four days from now, I'll be back and everyone will be available that day, I've checked. Does that work for you?'

She nodded:

'Yes.'

'You'll be able to pack your boxes the same day while we load your furniture into the van. I'll help you.'

She interrupted:

'No, I'll go first. I'll go the day before to get everything ready, I don't want to screw anything up.'

'But you don't have a lot of stuff there, do you? Clothes and some pictures? It'll only take a couple of hours, especially if there are a few of us.'

I didn't like the idea of her being alone with the Guy, especially after she'd told him they were no longer together, but she was sure of herself, there was no danger.

'Now that I'm certain I'm leaving he can say whatever he wants, it won't get to me.'

I tried one last time.

'He's not going to try and stop you? What if he's drunk again?'

'I'll deal with that.'

'What if he tries to lock you in? I don't know, anything's possible.'

'I'm stronger than he is.'

I sighed. I hoped she was right.

'The good news is you'll be able to stay at the house the very first evening. Some of the furniture we ordered will already be at Clara's, she'll bring it over to your place as soon as you get there, and the rest will be delivered the next week. Meaning that in four days you'll have a house. Your very own. And a few days after that you'll have everything you need.'

She inhaled through her nostrils, a slow, calm breath:

'I can't wait.'

★

Did I feel the need to help her because I'd hurt her a few years earlier and was now trying to repair that hurt? I don't think so because she had hurt me too and I have no regrets about what I said in that bookshop where she'd showed up by surprise, because my hurt and hers are linked, because they're twinned, without separation, without boundaries, I have no regrets because what had hurt her was me expressing my own hurt, I can't regret it because without this common Hurt, this Hurt that is neither hers nor mine but entirely ours, none of what was happening, between Paris and Athens, at a distance, through our phone screens, would have been possible.

What I do know is that doing all I could to help her was a matter of absolute necessity for me, and that this absolute necessity had me *on the verge of tears*.

★

Virginia Woolf's book *A Room of One's Own* takes as its starting point a series of lectures on the topic of women and literature, given by the author in 1928.

The power and originality of Woolf's book come from the fact that she refuses at first to tackle these two topics from the most expected angles: famous women writers, their style, the role of women in literary institutions or the revolutions they've brought about in terms of form.

Woolf writes: 'When you asked me to speak about women and fiction I sat down on the banks of a river and began to wonder what the words meant. They might mean simply a few remarks about Fanny Burney; a few more about Jane Austen; a tribute to the Brontës and a sketch of

Haworth Parsonage under snow; some witticisms if possible about Miss Mitford; a respectful allusion to George
Eliot; a reference to Mrs Gaskell and one would have done.'

Instead, Woolf made a much more radical proposal: she
drew up a practical programme that would enable women
to write books, faced with the limitations imposed on
them by their place in society, domestic tasks, isolation,
motherhood, marriage. Woolf replaces formal questions
with a material one, affirming that in order to write, a
woman needs above all two things:

– a room of her own that she can lock, so that she can
write undisturbed by family members;

– an income of £500, enabling her to live without worries.

Virginia Woolf answers a literary question with financial
and material concerns.

A room, a space, walls, a key, money: this is also, one
hundred years later, what my mother needed, not to
become a writer, but to become a freer, happier woman.

Woolf had understood, one hundred years earlier, that
freedom is not first and foremost an aesthetic and sym-
bolic issue, but a material and practical one. That freedom
has a price.

★

When I set out to write this book and tell the story of my mother's escape, my plan was to note in the margins the sums of money that had been necessary to bring it about. I wanted to provoke literature. I wanted this work to resemble in its form and appearance a document as common as a sales invoice, in other words the opposite of what literature often claims to be: noble, pure and disinterested.

I wanted, like Virginia Woolf with her income of five hundred pounds, to establish a concrete sum that would reflect the cost of a life and its possibility.

To this end, I'd written in the margins of the manuscript: *Amount advanced by Didier: 200 euros, Fridge: 500 euros, Gas cooker: 300 euros, Taxi to escape: 15 euros, Deposit on the house: 1,100 euros, Transfer for the first months of her New Life: 2,000 euros, etc.*

Just as in *Who Killed My Father* I had tried to introduce into literature the names of the men and women politicians and successive reforms that had affected my father's body, in this book I tried to introduce into literature money in the strictest and most explicit sense.

And then I stopped. Strangely, the numbers made the book ugly and unreadable. Above all, they gave the bizarre impression that I was blaming my mother for these sums.

They blurred the reading.

Can literature say everything?

If so, then I've failed.

If not, then literature is not enough.

★

One last remark: the story I'm telling is not a *homage to escape*. I can already see you thinking: Escaping is so beautiful! What a brave woman!

But you're wrong.

Because that's not enough.

When you read this story you must also ask yourself: Why do some people escape when others don't have to?

Why do some people always have to run, when others can sleep?

Why do some people always have to struggle, when others can make the most of things?

You must also ask yourself:

How many disappointments are there for every escape?

How many sacrificed lives are there for each life saved?

Because escape is a burden

Because escape is a burden

And much later
perhaps
it generates Beauty.

*

I returned to Paris. The plane landed in the late afternoon and I ran through the airport corridors to the train station. I ran faster and faster despite the weight of the suitcase in my hand, I was sweating.

I got on the regional train and waited for it to leave: at the end of the journey I was going to see my mother again, physically, for the first time since her escape.

An hour later I was standing in front of the door of my flat. I counted to three, *one, two, three*, and rang the bell.

My mother opened the door. Seeing her appear surrounded by the bookcases and all the objects I live with, I tried to hide my emotion; finding her once again so real after days of watching her on my phone screen was incredible, my brain couldn't adapt to this new situation and recreated the screen between us in my mind. I touched her hands to make sure she wasn't just a vision or a ghost. I was winded from running and the sound of my breathing rang in my ears.

I asked her:

'Are you okay?'

And she replied:

'Yes, I'm fine.'

I remembered that this was the question I'd asked her immediately after she'd managed to escape. I remembered that when she answered, at that moment, her voice, her words, her silences were blanketed by fatigue. Now she spoke in a way that was both light and resolute.

I thought: *She's crossed over to the other side.*

I started to cry and she teased me tenderly:

'As usual, I'm laughing and you're crying!'

I put my suitcase down and when I straightened up I saw that she'd put on make-up and done her hair for my arrival; when she chased my father out of the house where I'd grown up, a few years earlier, it was the first thing she'd done: put on make-up, I know I've already said it but I want to say it again.

On this day when we finally met up, in my little flat under the roof, surrounded by the sky, I told her she was beautiful; she whispered *thank you*. She blushed and to hide her embarrassment she showed me her little dog who was running circles around us:

'That's Pocket! He's a cutey too, isn't he? He couldn't wait to see you again he told me!'

I knelt down to pet him.

My mother pointed to the coffee table behind us: she'd laid out two small glasses and a carton of fruit juice, as well as some biscuits. I sat down in the armchair across from her:

'All ready for the move tomorrow?'

'Sure am, I went to the Guy's place this morning, my boxes are ready, everything's folded and packed. It only took me three hours. I'm happy.'

'How did he behave?'

'He just stood there. He was like a zombie watching me pack my things. He even asked if I needed help taping the boxes. You should have seen him so dismal and all! He said: Hang on Monique I'll help you.'

I needed one last reassurance:

'Are you sure nothing's going to happen tomorrow? I mean, he's not going to get angry or try to get you to change your mind at the last minute? Maybe when he sees the van something will snap and he'll lose it?'

She pursed her lips and pushed them forward in a sign of certainty:

'No, you'll see. When he hasn't been drinking he doesn't speak. And when there are strangers around he's even nice, wants to come across as likeable. Just like your dad.'

That too was a mystery I'd never understood: why,

in my childhood, my father was so polite and hospitable to the people who visited us at home, always ready to help them, always smiling, always quick to sacrifice his own time and pleasure for them, only to lose his temper and turn violent once he was alone with his family, suddenly attacking my mother or her relatives, because he knew that she was attached to them and that she'd be hurt by these attacks, he said her parents were nothing but

dirty Jews,

lousy Yids,

even though they weren't Jewish, simply because in his world and in his mind antisemitism was a way of expressing disgust and hatred.

My mother went on:

'And anyway, even if the Guy tries something tomorrow, I can hold my own. I've told you, no one's going to walk over me any more. And what's more, I've got my children to protect me.'

★

The day of the move arrived. I woke up in the hotel room where I'd spent the night to let my mother stay in my flat one last time before she left. As soon as I opened my eyes, I called my sister and her husband to see if they'd managed to collect the van, if everything had gone smoothly. It had, they'd left their place very early that morning, before sunrise. In fact they'd been in Paris for a while now, my sister told me, they'd started dismantling the furniture and loading the boxes into the van. My mother was with them, her voice was cheerful, she came to the telephone and said to me:

'Take your time waking up, drink your coffee in peace and come join us after that, we didn't want to tell you we were going to start so early because I didn't want you to set your alarm, I wanted you to get some rest. I know how much you hate the mornings!'

I protested, weakly:

'I could have got up early for once . . .'

'Don't worry, it was a plot for your own good! See you when you get here!'

I got ready, drank a couple of cups of coffee in the hotel room, and took the metro to join them.

Outside the weather was glorious, warm, the sun heated the surface of my skin. I arrived at the building. The van was parked on the pavement with its doors open wide, covered with multicoloured logos.

I gave my mother a big hug. My sister and her husband were there, her husband covered in sweat from all the lugging he'd been doing. The friend I'd asked to come and help had also arrived, he came down the stairs carrying some planks of wood.

And then without thinking, without looking for him, I turned my head and saw in a corner, between two walls, observing the scene from a distance, the man my mother had been staying with.

The Guy.

The one who'd been mistreating her all these years.

And when I saw him, this is what I'm getting at, when I saw him something extraordinary and disconcerting happened, something I couldn't have anticipated; when my eyes fell on him, I didn't feel anger or hatred as I'd expected, I didn't feel rage, I didn't feel any of that, just profound astonishment, and that astonishment gave rise to a question: how could such a puny, insignificant little being, with a shrimpy body and the face of a rat, how could a being so devoid of strength and stature have been the source of such violence? What happened?

I couldn't take my eyes off him.

I nodded at him from a distance, I didn't approach, but looking at him I suddenly began to think that maybe this man was neither guilty nor responsible for what he had done, that he himself had been the element through which a violence had passed that was bigger than him and not easily explained, the violence of his upbringing, the violence of his social class, the violence of living in a relationship, the violence of male domination, I began to think that maybe this man was the product of one or rather several intertwined situations over which he had no control, exactly as my mother had herself been violent when she lived with my father and was his prisoner, exactly as I had been violent with her in turn, I began to think, looking at this weak and pathetic-looking man, and against all expectation or anticipation on my part, that maybe he was innocent, innocent not in the sense that he inspired sympathy or affection in me, far from it, but innocent in the conceptual, pure sense, in the sense that nothing in him demonstrated a capacity *to do*, *to undertake*; he looked like someone who only reflects and reproduces the world around him, not someone who creates or brings anything into being, and I thought that maybe what I was taught by the innocence of this man, whom I nevertheless detested and disdained, was the innocence of everyone, innocence as a generalised condition.

What was this man telling me about the human condition? Looking at him, I thought that once he was alone, he could no longer be violent.

I saw him as pathetic.

I saw him as a sad case.

I felt a kind of pity for him, but I still didn't go anywhere near him.

I turned to my mother.

'You happy?'

'You bet I'm happy!'

I helped her carry down two or three last little bags,
everything else had already been packed into the van over
the course of the morning, there was hardly anything left
to do. I offered to order something for us all to eat. My
sister's husband answered that they didn't have time, they
had to head right back up to the Nord department, he
had to be at work early the next morning on a motorway
construction site; he was only twenty-five but I could
already see his body exhausted from work.

My sister came up to me:

'This is good, Mum's going to like it in the village.
There's lots to do, walks and workshops organised by the
town council. She won't be bored.'

I agreed:

'Yeah, she's happy to be going there.'

Awkward silence.

'You remember when we were both learning Spanish
at school and we used to say nasty things about Mum in
front of her without her understanding?'

I remembered.

'That was fun. But I think she suspected what we were saying.'

My sister fell silent again.

I searched around for something to say, but couldn't come up with anything.

'Will you come see us in the Nord now that we're all there? I've got an extra room so you can stay with us if you like. Just let me know.'

I said yes, I'd come, even though I knew I probably wouldn't. My sister looked around:

'Well, I guess we should be going. Mum, you ready?'

My mum raised both thumbs and smiled. I said goodbye and they all got in the cab of the van, my mum, my sister and her husband. The engine rumbled and started up, the van pulled away and disappeared among the other vehicles, getting further and further away; I watched it go. The fountain on my right covered the sounds of the city.

★

She got settled in. The remaining furniture and appliances were delivered on schedule, all in good condition. My mother was fifty-five years old, she was living alone for the first time in her life, without children, without a man, without anyone to look after or attend to round the clock, and that too I want to say again: *My mother was fifty-five years old, she was living alone for the first time in her life, without children, without a man, without anyone to look after or attend to round the clock.* I continued to call her every day while she got used to her new surroundings and made the transition. But even when our calls grew further apart, we continued to talk several times a week, which had never been the case before that. Her escape had brought us closer together.

She said: I'm so happy! I wake up when I want, I do what I want, no one's here to tell me what to do!

I replied that I found it so unfair that she'd had to wait so long to experience that, but she corrected me:

'It's because I've had such a hard time of things that I'm happier now! I don't care about the past! I can't stand people who weep about their past!'

And I said: You're right, you're right.

And I thought: She's stronger than me.

She sent me photos and videos of her and her dog in her living room, in the silence and calm of the afternoon, her windows open, the countryside in the distance. She commented: We're doing good! She shared with me the selfies in front of the mirror where she tried on different outfits, she told me about men she'd seen in the streets and found handsome, and asked me for money to buy herself some nice underwear, knickers, she persevered in being reborn, like someone who regains their senses after an accident and rediscovers functions their body thought it had forgotten.

(In fact, when she showed me the house in more detail with her phone camera I was disappointed, I found it cramped and run-down, I talked to Didier about it and he said: Look, if she chose it and she tells you she's happy, that's what counts, right? And he was right, I had to be careful not to steamroller her while trying to help her, sometimes there's only a fine line between the two.)

Two months after her move, she came back to Paris for a couple of days. I let her use my flat and she exclaimed:

'Ah, now I've got a pied-à-terre in Paris and a house in the country, like a bigwig!'

I'd bought some champagne for her visit. I opened it, we drank some, and for two hours she told me about her house. She sang, she did imitations of the people in the village she'd only just met; seeing her so happy, I started to think back to her old life and the times:

When she lived with my father and for no reason he'd crank the volume on the television up to max and demand that we keep quiet, or else he'd blow up.

My mother said to me, with a defeated look on her

face, *That's really not right of him to do that, he's got a screw loose or something, you'd think he was a psychopath in a film.*

When he'd repeated the same scene on Christmas Eve, when he'd put on some dumb variety show all evening and stopped us from talking to each other, from dancing.

The next day she'd said to me, vexed: He just got a kick out of ruining our Christmas. I could see it in his eyes.

When he'd go off to the café and she'd have to wait for him for dinner, even if she was hungry. He was the master of time: he decided, she waited.

When she'd say to me: I don't know why your father's in such a foul mood again today.

When he'd invite his friends over for a pastis in the evening and she couldn't take it any longer, because she wanted peace and quiet and the more my father and his friends drank, the louder they'd comment on the bodies of the women they saw on TV, Look at the knockers on that one, and what an arse!

When she'd say to me: I liked it so much when your father worked at least I had some peace he wasn't here all day long.

When she suffocated.

When, the first time we'd gone on holiday without him, she'd said to me: You see how much nicer I am without your father around? It's because he stresses me out that I become as mean as he is.

When she suffocated.

And then those scenes with the man she'd stayed with in Paris, scenes I didn't experience directly but which she told me about afterwards:
When he drank.
When he insulted her.
When he insulted my brothers and sisters,
and insulted me.
My mother's voice: *You can do anything to me but not that, you can't attack my children.*
When she suffered but hid it.
When she was afraid to eat because she knew he'd hold it against her.

When she suffered but hid it.

Now that was over.

She was alone.

She was free.

II

It's now three years since her escape across the city, maybe two. Time has accelerated, where did it go, the fact is I haven't yet had the chance to go see her in the village, I haven't seen her house for myself, but she continues to come here to Paris, she comes almost every month, and when she's here she never stops saying how wonderful, how amazing it is.

She even sees the Guy from time to time, she says no when he invites her over, she doesn't want to spend any more than an hour in his company, but she agrees to have a drink sometimes, when he insists, she says he no longer has any power over her, she says, as I understood on the day of the move, that violence is never engendered by a person but by a situation, so she keeps her distance – one single evening she makes the mistake of agreeing to spend the weekend in the flat where she used to stay with him. Right away it's the same old scene: he drinks, he drinks, and he insults her, he tells her that she disgusts him, that she's a whore, a bitch, a slut. She writes to me to ask if she can go straight to my friend Giovanni's flat, she has the key to his place, he's often away and that's where she sleeps when she comes to see me or simply to enjoy the atmosphere in the city.

After that she'll never sleep at the Guy's place again. Ever. But she still talks to him, she says:

'It's pointless to be angry with people, it's a waste of time.'

★

Most of the time I see her on the terrace of a café in Saint-Germain-des-Prés, or at my place, in the living room that was hers during the ten or so days of her metamorphosis and her escape.

She is a woman who smiles.

Of course the bond between us is no longer as strong as it was when she was suffering, nothing brings people together as much as shared suffering, but the things we've been through have opened a breach into the present: a lasting tenderness that nothing seems able to break forms the foundation of our meetings and discussions.

I go in quest of her adolescence and youth, I ask her

questions that would have been unimaginable just a few years earlier, I've become my mother's archaeologist:

'I want to know everything. We can start anywhere. Tell me what you did on a day like today when you were sixteen, for example.'

'A day like today? I was probably getting ready to go out to a dance. I loved that, in those days you went to dances to meet boys.'

'And did you meet many of them?'

'I fought with them too when they got on my nerves. I was a tomboy, it was better not to mess with me.'

I laugh.

She is a woman who makes me laugh.

★

She's no longer my mother. Maybe that's why the bond between us has become possible. The only time I get bored with her is when she comes to Paris with my youngest brother: him being there forces her to play the predictable role of a mother, she talks about how much a little cousin I've never met weighed when he was born, she argues with my brother the way I argued with her in my early years.

Now I make a point of seeing her only when she's

alone: then she once again becomes something other than a mother, she's a friend, a woman who talks about her own desires, wishes and dreams.

I also try hard to be something other than a son, to be more, to be better.

A friend tells me: You've got to add a touch of friendship to your relationship with your mum.

★

Then one afternoon I get a call on my phone.

The man calling is a famous German theatre director. He says,

it's like this,

he'd like to create a performance based on a book about her, about my mother, which I wrote and published the previous year, the book is called *A Woman's Battles and Transformations*, in it I tell the story of how she escaped from my father after more than twenty years with him, twenty years of suffocation, in it I tried to retrace her first escape, before her arrival at *the Guy*'s place in Paris, the director tells me that he'd like to put his performance on in one of the biggest theatres in Germany, in Hamburg, an immense, cathedral-like hall in which one thousand two hundred people sit in the dark facing the stage. He tells me that he already has ideas, he imagines something spectacular, something extravagant, a group of German feminist musicians from the 1980s, the group no longer exists but the musicians would be willing to get together again for the show and compose new songs, he says he imagines Eva Mattes, a legendary actress who appeared in the films of Rainer Werner Fassbinder, to play my mother, another actress who would turn into a butterfly and fly fifteen metres above the audience to symbolise the struggles and victories of a woman who seemed condemned never to escape, he explains that his approach won't be realism but fantasy, with a brand of fantasy that matches the dreams and reinventions of this woman in the book that moved him, and listening to him describe his project a thought crosses my mind: I'll go there with my mother.

Suddenly I'm struck by the idea that I could take her with me, and this journey could be a new chapter in her story, a new odyssey of Revenge: that she, who's spent a large part of her life in the shadows, in tiny villages in the north of France and then in a gloomy caretaker's flat in Paris, kept at home by men, hidden, made invisible, silenced by all the forms of Power, that she who repeated throughout my childhood *Nobody cares about little people like us*, that she, a woman, poor, a mother of five at just over thirty, with no qualifications, no career, could see her life acted out onstage, in front of a crowd of people she doesn't know, her life portrayed by great actresses of the German theatre, lit by stage lights, set to music, held up as a model.

I thank the director. I say yes, of course I accept his proposition. He adds that if I wish, the theatre will set tickets aside for my mother and me.

I say thank you, thank you, and I hang up.

I wait for my mother's next trip to Paris. My eagerness slows down time, it's when I want it to go by that it stops, and when I want it to stop that it passes in a flash, I count the days, I talk about my plan to my friends, Didier, Geoffroy, Tash, Giovanni, I want to be sure that I'm doing things right, that I'm not making a mistake, and one afternoon she's finally there, back, facing me, on the terrace of the same café in Saint-Germain-des-Prés where we always meet.

I announce:

'I've got a surprise for you.'

'A surprise?'

'Yes, but only if you're up for it. You decide.'

'Tell me.'

'A few days ago I got a call from a director in Germany. He'd like to stage a play about your life. I thought we could go there together. Would you like that?'

She gasps:

'Would I like that? Have you seen my hair? I don't want people to see me all grey like this!'

I laugh:

'It's months from now, we'll have time to take care of that . . . So do you want to go?'

She looks at me as if I were a lunatic asking a senseless question:

'Yes. Of course I do.'

★

The day of the performance and our trip approaches. She talks about it a lot and as we talk I become fully aware of all the dimensions of our imminent departure for Germany: my mother has never crossed a border in her life, she's never seen a country other than her own, apart from one afternoon on a boat off the coast of England with her school, just a few kilometres from the port town in the north of France where she grew up, she's never walked down a street and heard a language other than her own, she's never been in contact with another culture, another civilisation, she's fifty-seven years old and she's never taken a plane in her life, she's never seen the sky from the inside and the earth from the sky, she's never slept in a hotel room, she's never been to the theatre, except to see a few school plays when she was around ten or twelve, she's never seen a real performance directed by a real director, of course she's never seen a show in which she's the main protagonist, she's never been invited to travel by an institution the way artists or politicians can be.

For her all these things we were getting ready to do together would be a succession of First Times.

A war against an army of Nevers.

★

She met me outside my building around noon. She'd put on perfume, her hair was a resplendent blonde. The week before she'd spent an afternoon at a hairdresser's in the fourteenth arrondissement.

When I came out she exclaimed:

'No comparison with the dyes you get in the supermarket!'

On this Departure day she put her little suitcase on the pavement and spun around.

'What do you think?'

'You're perfect.'

'I'm the queen of Paris, don't forget, that's what you said to me one day.'

I kissed her on the cheek, took her suitcase and we walked to the nearest regional train station. On the way I asked her:

'Did you sleep well?'

'Not too well, I was excited about leaving.'

'Have you got your identity card?'

'Yes, look.'

She'd prepared a folder on which she'd written: *Trip to Hamburg*, with her ID, but also her social security card, her family record book, the printout of her plane ticket, a letter she'd written for everyone involved in the show, way too many documents.

(And looking at the letter I could see that she must have spent entire days thinking about it and drafting it to make sure that there were no mistakes and that the writing was as perfect as possible. I could see from the words she used that she'd looked up, weighed, and compared expressions to try to write in good French. She asked me:

'Can you read it on the plane and tell me what you think?'

I remembered how, when I was in high school, she used to ask me to write official letters for her, no doubt feeling that as I was the first one in the family to make it as far as the lycée, I had mastered the language and would therefore know how to use it to convince a civil servant to grant us funding or some other assistance. I remembered her breathing over my shoulder as I concentrated and wrote, and how our relationship was suddenly reversed.)

At the airport, everything was new for her: going through security, putting her things in the plastic bins to be scanned, taking out liquids. I'd warned her to take only small bottles but she had a large moisturising spray for her face, a tube of body shimmer and a bottle of conditioner.

I told her she'd have to throw them in the bin.

She looked at the screening officers, sure of herself:

'I'll tell them that they're just beauty products.'

I told her that wouldn't work and she stared at me in astonishment:

'What's wrong with carrying body shimmer?'

★

The plane took off. I'd selected a seat beside the window for her when I checked us in so she could enjoy the view: she sat down, pressed her face against the oval window and didn't move for the whole flight. She was hypnotised by the immensity in front of her, by the light. She turned to me from time to time to say, in a younger voice than usual:

'It's beautiful!'

She took out her phone and filmed the clouds rolling by and the blue sky around us.

'I'm going to show that to little Arthur your sister's boy he's not going to believe it!'

In Hamburg too she marvelled at everything, she wanted to take in the tiniest details of everything she laid eyes on: Look, the police cars aren't the same as they are in France! But the houses are similar! The same roofs! There are towels in the hotel room! I took mine for nothing! There's even free shampoo!

I promised her we'd go on other trips together.

She added:

'When I was little my biggest dream was to travel around the world.'

★

At eight in the evening she was waiting for me in the hotel foyer to leave for the theatre.

I saw her from a distance, clenching her fists and shifting her weight from one leg to the other.

'I'm a bit stressed.'

'Don't worry, it's going to be fine. Everyone wants to meet you.'

We walked to the theatre, which was just next door. She squeezed my arm with hers. I could smell her perfume. Her skin shone. The director welcomed us.

'Mum, this is Falk Richter. He's the one who created the show.'

He held out his hand and said to her in French, with a slight German accent:

'Delighted to meet you. I'm glad you're here tonight. I really admire you for what you've been through; you're a courageous woman.'

I'd told him that's what Didier had said to her the day she escaped, and that she'd been flattered. He remembered, and was repeating it to please her. I was touched by this gesture, by such thoughtfulness.

She nodded:

'Thank you. I've always told my children that the most important thing is courage.'

She was being careful how she spoke, trying to control her northern accent, I could tell. I wanted to tell her that she had the right to be herself, that she shouldn't try to be someone else, but after all wasn't I doing the same thing, on other levels? I too modified my attitude towards strangers, towards the people who were crowding round the doors of the theatre that evening, towards the ushers, towards the booksellers who were displaying my books. Who doesn't change the way they are in front of others?

Maybe she wasn't feeling pain or shame, but pleasure,

the pleasure of playing at being someone else, and so, for a few moments, of becoming someone else.

The director asked her:

'Would you be willing to come and take a bow with us onstage at the end of the show?'

I'd warned her, she was ready.

'Yes, yes. I mean, if you like.'

He whispered:

'I'd love that.'

Then, with a smile:

'We'll take our bows in order of importance. First me, the least important, the director. Then your son the writer. And you at the end, the most important.'

When he said this she opened her eyes wide and replied with a look of deep astonishment:

'Really? I'm important?'

She couldn't contain that sentence, it came out of her, pure, true, absolute.

'Of course you are! Look at all these people who've come to hear your story.'

That threw her off completely. I hugged her.

The director excused himself, he had to go talk to the cast and crew before the performance started, he'd meet us later.

I turned to her and said:

'You still okay?'

She nodded to me. She couldn't speak. And in my head I played back her astonishment again and again:

Really? I'm important?

★

We sat down on purple velvet-covered seats under an enormous chandelier, surrounded by gold trim and the whispering of the audience – a special kind of whispering, reflecting the privilege of those to whom art is addressed, muted, subdued, even in whispering there's a difference of class.

The lights went down and the show began. The actors didn't speak in French but in German, I whispered in my mother's ear so she could follow along and understand which moment in her life each scene dealt with.

As I said, the play was based on the book I'd written about her break-up with my father, her escape before the other escape from the man she'd stayed with in Paris, and onstage we saw sequences from her life between the ages of twenty-five and forty-five, how she'd met my father, how in order to win her over he'd led her to believe he'd be different from the other men she'd known, before behaving exactly like them, insulting her, mistreating her. I was afraid that the confrontation between her and these scenes of violence could hurt her, and I said to her in a low voice, so that she could put what she was seeing into perspective:

'Don't forget that this is theatre, of course it's exaggerated . . .'

She sought my gaze in the darkness:

'It's not exaggerated at all, that's exactly what it was like!'

She laughed.

Nothing could hurt her any more.

When, on the stage, after a series of arguments with the man who played my father, we saw the actress who played my mother's role decide to fill plastic bags with his belongings and throw them out of the window onto the street, telling him never to return, the way my mother had done in real life a few years earlier, she, my mother, turned to me and pulled her arms in towards her: *Yes Yes Yes!* as if she'd been afraid that the actress wouldn't be able to escape, as if seeing her past re-enacted made that past present again, in other words prey to contingencies and chance events, as if the present of the show could have changed her past.

I would have liked this depiction of my mother never to end, so she could contemplate herself for eternity, so I could contemplate her contemplating herself, and so she could feel my gaze on her and the gaze of others both on her body and on her story, in an infinite play of mirrors.

The curtain fell and the audience around us applauded.

At that moment I felt excitement and apprehensiveness surge like spasms from my mother's body, just a few centimetres from me. Her eyes were shining. She knew that in a matter of seconds thousands of eyes would be upon her.

And I thought: *Here we go.*

I'd been fantasising about this moment for months, Freud says somewhere that fantasising is a waking dream, a daytime dream.

And the applause was so loud, I swear, when the actors and actresses came back to take their bows it was so loud that it made the ground vibrate beneath our feet.

I thought: *One more revenge for her.*

If freedom isn't revenge then it isn't freedom, that's what I believe.

One of the main actors in the show, the one who played the role of the narrator, took hold of a microphone handed to him by a technician and asked for silence in the theatre.

My heart raced: *Soon her turn. Soon hers.*

The actor called Falk first, as planned, to come up and take a bow.

Falk went up onstage.

Applause.

Soon her turn. Soon hers.

The actor called me. *See you in a sec*, I whispered to my mother as I stood up, and joined the others onstage.

And then, as the applause continued, the actor-narrator asked for silence once again and announced: *We have one more surprise for you tonight. Someone special has come to see the show . . . Ladies and gentlemen, please give a very big hand for the author's mother, Monique.*

Everyone in the theatre stood up. In a single movement, like one body. They applauded more fervently, louder and louder, one thousand two hundred people cheering enthusiastically, shouting hurrah, whistling in her honour.

My mother smiled, I could see her from a distance, stage fright made her movements less smooth and more awkward, but she was happy, that too I swear, she was happy.

She approached the stage, the actor helped her up, she thanked him, she caught her breath and finally she turned towards the audience who were screaming her name.

She stepped forward.

Not far enough, she didn't dare, out of shyness, out of ignorance of theatrical conventions.

I pushed her slightly on the back to get her to go a little closer to the edge of the stage.

The cries of joy in the hall redoubled.

The applause continued, on and on, and I thought: *Maybe it'll never stop.*

I could see the back of my mother's neck a few metres in front of me, the hair she'd had dyed and styled for the occasion, her body freer and freer, the fist she'd raised to the sky, and I repeated to myself: *She's won.*

She's won.

III

Two weeks after we got back from Germany, she took a train from the north of France to come spend the afternoon with me in Paris.

I wanted her to tell me, looking back, how she'd felt, how she'd experienced the show and then everything that happened that evening from the inside: the strangers who'd crowded around her at the exit to talk to her and get her to sign books and programmes, others who'd asked if they could take selfies with her, the party organised by the theatre during which the musicians from the show commented on the songs they'd written during the rehearsals, inspired by her, by her story and her struggles, based on her life and her experiences – one of the songs, her favourite, was called 'The Queen of Paris'.

(Another anecdote: I'd thought she'd be bored at this party because no one or almost no one spoke French, and everything she heard had to be translated sentence by sentence. I'd reserved a table for the two of us at a restaurant where I'd thought we'd

go afterwards; I'd imagined that we'd escape at some point so she could feel more comfortable, but she hadn't wanted to leave the party. I'd asked her:

'Do you want to stay? It doesn't bother you that everyone's speaking German and English?'

And she'd said:

'Of course I want to stay, I'm having the time of my life!'

We'd finally left at three in the morning, our ears ringing, starving, and walked through the freezing night to the nearest McDonald's, the one at Hamburg station, the only place where you could still get something to eat in the middle of the night, and we'd eaten in silence, exhausted, in the smell of fried food, lit by fluorescent lights, exhausted but saturated with memories and images, fulfilled.)

Two weeks later, then, she knocked on the door of my flat; I was waiting for her. I got up, opened the door and asked her to come in.

I'd prepared some questions for her. I knew she'd shown some of her neighbours in her village the video of her going up onstage to thunderous applause – my sister had told me.

I asked her how she was doing, what she'd been up to in the few days since we last saw each other, but just as she was about to answer she spotted a copy of the book that had inspired the German performance, *A Woman's Battles and Transformations*, on one of my bookshelves.

She went over, picked it up and examined it.

'I've changed a lot again since you wrote this book. You'll have to write that one day! I've changed again.'

I told her she was right:

'It's true. It's true. And I will.'

At the time when she said those words, half in jest, half serious, I was trying to write another book. That book explored the story of my relationship with my older brother, who died from alcohol at thirty-eight.

Since then, I've put that account of our relationship on hold to write this new chapter of my mother's life, of her metamorphoses.

Through her, I've discovered the pleasure of writing in the service of someone else.

I've become acquainted with the delight that accompanies disappearance, self-effacement, becoming just a glimpse into the story of a destiny other than my own.

This book you are reading is, in a certain sense, commissioned by my mother.

I didn't decide on it, I didn't plan it.

I wasn't the first one to get the idea.

Nothing in literature has ever given me so much joy.

References

Hélène Cixous, *Eve Escapes: Ruins and Life*. Translated by Peggy Kamuf, Polity Press, 2012.

Didier Eribon, *The Life, Old Age, and Death of a Working-Class Woman*. Translated by Michael Lucey, Penguin, 2025.

Jamaica Kincaid, *My Brother*, Vintage, 1998.

Georg Simmel, 'The Poor', in *On Individuality and Social Forms*. Translated by Claire Jacobson, The University of Chicago Press, 1971.

Virginia Woolf, *A Room of One's Own*, Hogarth Press, 1929.